Why are fish like lions?

camilla de la Bedoyere

Miles
KeLLY

First published in 2011 by Miles Kelly Publishing Ltd
Harding's Barn, Bardfield End Green, Thaxted,
Essex, CM6 3PX, UK

2 4 6 8 10 9 7 5 3 1

Publishing Director Belinda Gallagher
Creative Director Jo Cowan
Editorial Director Rosie McGuire
Editor Claire Philip
Volume Designer Andrew Crowson
Cover Designer Kayleigh Allen
Image Manager Liberty Newton
Indexer Gill Lee
Production Manager Elizabeth Collins
Reprographics Anthony Cambray, Stephan Davis

ISBN 978-1-84810-457-0

Printed in China

British Library Cataloguing-in-Publication Data

A catalogue record for this book is
available from the British Library

ACKNOWLEDGEMENTS
The publishers would like to thank the following
artist who has contributed to this book:

Mike Foster (character cartoons)

All other artwork from the Miles Kelly Artwork Bank

The publishers would like to thank the following
sources for the use of their photographs:

Dreamstime.com 15 Johnandersonphoto;
21 Goodolga; 23 Naluphoto
Fotolia.com 4 Desertdiver; 9 cbpix
iStockphoto.com 29 Boris Tarasov
Rex Features 6 c.W. Disney/Everett/Rex Features
Shutterstock.com 7 bernd.neeser; 12 Rich Carey;
16 Levent Konuk; 18 A Cotton Photo; 25 tubuceo;
27 John A. Anderson

All other photographs are from:
digitalSTOCK, PhotoDisc

Every effort has been made to acknowledge the
source and copyright holder of each picture.
Miles Kelly Publishing apologises for any unintentional
errors or omissions.

Made with paper from a sustainable forest

www.mileskelly.net
info@mileskelly.net

www.factsforprojects.com

Self-publish your
children's book

buddingpress.co.uk

Contents

what is a coral reef?

Coral reefs are living structures that grow in the sea. They are built by millions of tiny animals, called coral polyps. When they die, new polyps grow on top. This builds up layers of coral rock over time. Some reefs, such as the Great Barrier Reef, are enormous and can be seen from the air.

Great Barrier Reef

Coral

Do trees grow underwater?

Trees do not grow underwater, but soft tree corals look like trees because they have branches. Coral reefs are sometimes called 'rainforests of the sea'. Like rainforests on land, coral reefs are important homes for millions of marine animals.

Soft tree coral

Big brains!

Octopuses are super smart animals that live near reefs. They are experts at finding prey hiding in rocky crevices.

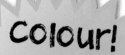

Colour!

Choose your favourite fish from this book. Copy it onto paper and colour it in.

How do coral polyps feed?

Coral polyps live in hard, stony cups and feed on tiny animals that drift by in the water. They catch food with tiny stingers on their tentacles, as do jellyfish, which are in the same animal family as coral polyps.

can turtles swim far?

Turtles go on very long journeys across the sea to feed, mate or lay their eggs. Female turtles always return to the same beach to lay their eggs. How they find their way is still a mystery, but they don't seem to get lost!

Discover

Use an atlas to find out which country beginning with 'A' is near the Great Barrier Reef.

Turtles from *Finding Nemo*

when does a fish look like a stone?

When it is a stonefish! Stonefish are almost impossible to see when they are lying flat and still on the seabed. Their colours blend in with the rocky and sandy surfaces.

Stonefish

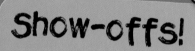

Show-offs!

Cuttlefish can change colour! In just a few seconds, a cuttlefish can flash colours of red, yellow, brown or black.

Do seahorses gallop?

Seahorses are fish, not horses, so they cannot run or gallop! They are not very good swimmers so they wrap their tails around seaweed to stop ocean currents carrying them away.

why are fish like lions?

Lionfish

Some fish are like lions because they hunt for food at night. Lionfish hide among rocks in the day. As the sun sets, they come out to hunt for small animals to eat. They have amazing stripes and spines on their bodies. Their spines hold venom, which can cause very painful stings.

Dive but stay alive!

Divers can use cages to watch sharks safely. The divers wear masks and carry tanks that have air inside them so they can breathe underwater.

when do birds visit reefs?

Birds visit coral reef islands to build their nests. When their eggs hatch, the birds find plenty of fish at the reef to feed to their chicks. Albatrosses are large sea birds, so their chicks need lots of fish!

count

If an albatross chick needs to eat two big fish every day, how many fish will it eat in five days?

can slugs be pretty?

Yes they can! Like many coral reef animals, sea slugs have amazing colours and patterns. These warn other animals that they are harmful to eat. Most sea slugs are small, but some can grow to 30 centimetres in length.

Sea slugs

What lives on a reef?

A huge number of different animals live on or around reefs. They are home to fish of all shapes and sizes, including sharks. There are many other animals too – octopus, squid, slugs, sponges, starfish and urchins all live on reefs.

Black sea urchin

Sea turtle

Starfish

Do turtles lay eggs?

Yes, they do. Turtles spend most of their lives at sea, but lay their eggs on land. A female turtle digs a hole in the sand, and lays her round eggs inside it. When the eggs hatch, the baby turtles crawl back to the sea.

A sting in the tail!

Blue-spotted rays live in coral reefs and feed on shellfish, crabs and worms. They have stinging spines on their tails.

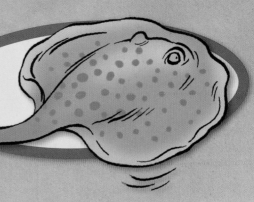

Measure

Every year coral reefs grow about 10 centimetres. How much have you grown in a year?

What do coral reefs need to grow?

The polyps that build up coral reefs need plenty of sunlight and clean water to grow. They mostly live in shallow water near land where sunlight can reach them.

Sea goldies

Bottlenose dolphins

Barracudas

Butterfly fish

Wobbegong shark

Whitetip reef shark

can parrots swim?

Of course not – parrots are birds that live in jungles! Parrotfish, however, are dazzling, colourful fish that swim around reefs, nibbling at the coral. They have beak-like mouths, which is why they are named after parrots.

Parrotfish

which animal looks like seaweed?

A type of seahorse called a leafy seadragon does! Its strange shape makes it hard to spot when it swims around seaweed, hiding it from big fish that might want to eat it.

Leafy seadragon

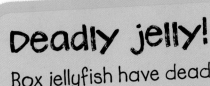

Think

Make up a story about a leafy seadragon and a parrotfish. Draw pictures to tell your story.

Do sponges help build reefs?

Sometimes – sponges are animals that bore, or dig, holes into coral. This can weaken a reef. However, when sponges die their bodies build up extra layers, which add to the reef structure.

Deadly jelly!

Box jellyfish have deadly stings on their tentacles. Divers and swimmers stay away from them.

Why does an octopus have eight arms?

Having eight arms allows an octopus to move quickly and grab food to eat. Each arm has suction cups that can grip onto things. An octopus grabs food with its eight strong arms, and pulls it towards its mouth.

MAKE
Draw lots of pictures of coral reef animals and stick them on a large piece of card to make a poster.

Blue-ringed octopus

Who looks after a seahorse's eggs?

Females lay the eggs, but the males look after them in a special pouch on the front of their bodies. This keeps the eggs safe from bigger fish that might eat them. When the eggs hatch, the babies swim out of the pouch.

Don't eat me!

Little coral polyps live next to each other, but they do not always get on. Sometimes one polyp might eat its neighbour!

Do christmas trees grow on reefs?

Christmas trees do not grow on reefs – but Christmas tree worms do! These little animals live in burrows inside the reef. The feathery, spiral parts we can see are called feeding tentacles.

Christmas tree worm

where do clownfish live?

Clownfish live in the tentacles of coral reef creatures called sea anemones. Like coral polyps, these strange-looking animals sting their prey. Clownfish have a slimy skin covering that protects them from the sting and allows them to live there unharmed.

Sea anemone

Hide

Invite some friends to join you in a game of hide and seek. Where could you hide?

Clownfish

see snakes? swim!

Snakes don't just live on land. Some of the world's most deadly snakes live in the sea but come onto land to lay their eggs.

can seashells be deadly?

The coneshell can be! The shell is just the animal's hard outer casing – it is the soft-bodied creature inside that is the dangerous part. Coneshells hunt other animals and attack by jabbing them with a deadly venom.

Coneshell

which shrimp likes to punch its prey?

Mantis shrimps may be small, but they can pack a big punch. They live in reefs near Australia and in the Pacific Ocean. They punch their prey to stun them, and then tuck in for a tasty meal.

can starfish be blue?

Most starfish are red or brown, but big blue ones live on some reefs. Starfish have small, tube-like feet on the undersides of their arms, which allow them to crawl over the reef. They have tiny eyes at the end of each arm, which can only see light or dark.

Starfish

Make

Make a map that shows where pirate treasure is buried on a coral island.

Do jellyfish wobble?

No, jellyfish may look like jelly, but they are living animals. They have long, stinging tentacles that hang below their bodies as they swim. Some jellyfish live around coral reefs, where there are plenty of fish to eat.

Box jellyfish

Fish hotspot!

There are more than 24,000 different types of fish in the world. Many of those live in or around coral reefs.

Why did pirates bury treasure on coral islands?

Pirates are believed to have buried stolen treasure so no one could find it. There are lots of stories about pirates who buried gold and precious stones on coral islands, but we don't know how true these tales are.

Why are corals different shapes?

The shape a coral grows into depends on the type of polyp it has. Where the coral grows on the reef is also important. Brain coral grows slowly and in calm water. Staghorn and elkhorn corals grow more quickly, and in shallow water.

Brain coral

Elkhorn coral

Staghorn coral

Are there butterflies in the sea?

There is a type of butterfly living in the sea – but it isn't an insect, it's a fish! Many butterfly fish have colourful spots and stripes to help make them hard to spot.

Butterfly fish

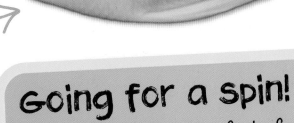

LOOK
Find out if you can see colours better in the dark or in the light.

Going for a spin!
Dolphins visit coral reefs to feast on fish. They jump out of the water and can even spin, though no one knows why they do it!

Can fish see in the dark?

Many of animals can see in the dark! Lots of coral animals sleep during the day, but when the Sun goes down they come out to look for food or mates. Many of them, such as the red soldierfish, are much better at seeing in the dark than people are.

Which crab moves house?

Hermit crabs live inside borrowed shells and move house if they find a bigger, better one. They don't have their own shells so they have to find one to protect their soft bodies. Most hermit crabs choose snail shells to live in.

Hermit crab →

Why is some coral white?

Most coral is very colourful, until it dies and turns white or grey. There are many reasons why corals are dying. Dirty water is one of the most important reasons. Water that is too warm is also bad for polyps.

Damaged coral

Slow-grow!

Giant clams can grow to be enormous — up to 150 centimetres long! They can live for 70 years.

Who looks after coral reefs?

Special ocean parks are set up to look after the animals that live on coral reefs. People are not allowed to catch the fish or damage the reef inside these protected areas.

Measure

Use a measuring tape to find out how long a giant clam is.

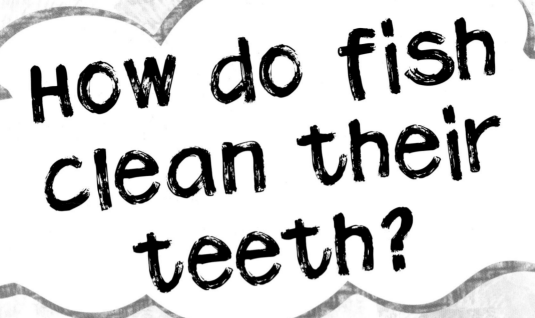

How do fish clean their teeth?

They get other fish to do it for them! Little fish, called wrasses, eat the bits of food stuck in the teeth of other fish, such as moray eels. The wrasses get a tasty meal and the moray eels get their teeth cleaned!

Moray eel

Whale shark

Are all sharks dangerous?

No, most sharks would never attack a person. Whale sharks are huge but they don't eat big animals. They swim through the water with their large mouths open. They suck in water and any little creatures swimming in it.

which crab wears boxing gloves?

Boxer crabs hold sea anemones in their claws, like boxing gloves. They wave them at any animals that come too close — the sight of the stinging tentacles warns other animals to stay away.

Brush

We don't have wrasses, so when you brush your teeth try hard to remove every tiny bit of food.

Wrasse

School's out!

A group of fish is called a shoal, or a school. Fish often swim in shoals because it helps them stay safe from bigger fish that might eat them.

Do sharks use hammers?

No, but some sharks have heads that look like hammers! These strange-looking sharks have wide, flattened heads. The shape might help them to find food, swim fast or change direction easily.

Hammerhead shark →

Do squid change colour?

Yes, squid and octopuses are able to change colour, so they can hide, or send messages to each other. They can change colour very quickly – in just one or two seconds!

Caribbean reef squid

world wonder

You can see the Great Barrier Reef from space! At over 2000 kilometres long, it is the largest structure ever built by living creatures

which fish are shocking?

Electric rays can shock other animals by making electric charges in their bodies. As they swim over other fish, they stun them with powerful jolts of electricity. The rays then eat their prey whole, headfirst!

Dress

We change the way we look with the clothes we wear. How quickly can you change clothes?

which fish is spiky?

Pufferfish are strange-looking, poisonous fish with sharp spines. When they feel scared, pufferfish blow up their bodies to make their spines stand on end. This makes them bigger and much harder to swallow.

Pufferfish with spines relaxed

Pufferfish with spines on end

March

Imagine you are a lobster on a long march. How far can you march before you get tired?

Why do lobsters march?

Coral reef spiny lobsters march to deep, dark water where they lay their eggs. They march through the night at the end of the summer. Thousands of lobsters join the march to reach a safe place to breed.

Clean teeth!

When fish such as sweetlips want their teeth cleaned, they swim to find wrasse fish and open their mouths.

Crown-of-thorns starfish

HOW do starfish eat their prey?

Starfish turn their mouths inside out to eat. The crown-of-thorns starfish kills coral by eating the soft polyps inside. Each of these large starfish can have up to 21 arms.

Quiz time

Do you remember what you have read about coral reefs? Here are some questions to test your memory. The pictures will help you. If you get stuck, read the pages again.

3. Why are fish like lions?

page 8

4. Do turtles lay eggs?

page 10

1. Do trees grow underwater?

page 5

5. Which animal looks like seaweed?

page 13

page 7

2. When does a fish look like a stone?

6. Who looks after a seahorse's eggs?

page 15

7. Where do clownfish live?

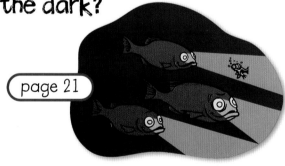

page 16

11. Which crab wears boxing gloves?

page 25

8. Do jellyfish wobble?

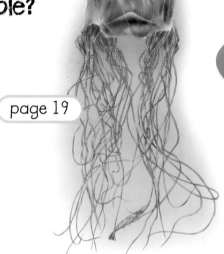

page 19

12. Which fish are shocking?

page 27

13. Why do lobsters march??

page 29

9. Can fish see in the dark?

page 21

10. Who looks after coral reefs?

page 23

Answers

1. No, but some corals have branches like trees
2. When it is a stonefish
3. Because they are hunters and come out to feed at night
4. Yes
5. The leafy sea dragon
6. The male seahorse
7. In the tentacles of sea anemones
8. No, they are living animals and aren't made from jelly
9. Yes – many such as the red soldierfish can see well in the dark
10. Special ocean parks
11. The boxer crab
12. Electric rays
13. They march to an area where they can breed or lay their eggs

index